Bibliographic information published by the German National Library:

The German National Library lists this publication in the National Bibliography; detailed bibliographic data are available on the Internet at http://dnb.dnb.de .

Imprint:

Copyright © 2017 GRIN Verlag
Print and binding: Books on Demand GmbH, Norderstedt Germany
ISBN: 9783668679375

Neha Tandon, Pankaj Bhambri

Novel Approach for Drug Discovery using Neural Network Back Propagation Algorithm

An Optimum Drug Discovery Approach

GRIN Verlag

GRIN - Your knowledge has value

Since its foundation in 1998, GRIN has specialized in publishing academic texts by students, college teachers and other academics as e-book and printed book. The website www.grin.com is an ideal platform for presenting term papers, final papers, scientific essays, dissertations and specialist books.

Content

CHAPTER 1
INTRODUCTION

1.1 INTRODUCTION TO ONTOLOGY

The types, properties and the interrelationships of the objects that are truly present within the specific domain of discourse are named formally within the ontology. The practical application of the philosophical ontology along with the taxonomy is considered along this path. The variables that are required for some set of calculations are provided by the ontology. Further various relationships are established amongst them. There is a movement of the data processing system towards the concept processing in the modern information systems. This means that the atomic part of data is at minimum the very essential part of the data. The translation is conveyed and the context that provides the various methods is also proposed. A structure that holds the knowledge related to a specified area with the help of related concepts and relations amongst them is known as the ontology process [1].

The capacity to evaluate the specific approach is the main objective here. The similar ideas are to be considered here within this approach. During the management of the abstractions within the ontologies, there is a same process followed by the semantic web explore area. For the purpose of conceptualizing knowledge, the ontologies provide a specific data structure. By involving completely different knowledge related to these concepts, new methods are to be generated here. As per the comparisons of the predefined criterion, the technology that is the best has to be selected here. The evaluation of ontology is a very important issue that needs to be addressed if there is a need to involve the ontologies within the semantic web and the various semantic-aware applications. There is a need of certain methods to access the ontologies within the multitude of clients that required a multitude. On the basis of this, the best method is selected as per the needs.

A complex structure that focuses on the analysis of variety of levels in regular manner is known as the ontology process. It is different from the methods that evaluate the ontology in a direct manner. When there is a need to transcendently automate the evaluation and not totally leaving the work on clients is the main focus here. There has been an involvement in the programmed learning methods for constructing the ontology which is completely a level-based method. There are different strategies included for various levels. There are all these levels that are defined at various levels. There is however a comparative analysis of these methods and there definitions are to be defined individually [2]:

- Lexical, vocabulary, or data layer: Within the ontology, the main highlight here is of the concepts, occasions, realities etc. there is a need of the vocabulary for representing such ideas. There is a need to include the examinations with the help of various sources related to the data related problem domains. Also the strategies such as the string similarity measures are involved within this level.

- Hierarchy or taxonomy: A is-a relation is developed amongst the concepts within the ontology in a regular manner. Although there is a need to provide variety of relations here, the is-a relation is important and will highlight the study of the specific evaluation efforts only [3].

- Other semantic relations: Apart from is-an there are various relations involved within the ontology. There is an independent evaluation of these relations. The measures such as precision and recall are to be incorporated with these measures.

3

- Context or application level: The huge collection of various ontologies involves smaller ontology as a part of them. With the help of various definitions within these ontologies, the ontology may be referenced. The context of this situation is required to be considered during its analysis. There is another aspect in which the ontology concept might be included. It involves the evaluation of the results achieved within various applications that affect the usage of ontology.

- Syntactic level: The ontology which has specific interest is required to be evaluated within this level in a manual manner. Within specific formal language, the ontology is depicted here. It requires to be matching the syntactic needs of the particular language. There is a need to consider the syntactic requirements, which involve the closeness of the natural-language documentation, evading of loops amongst the definitions and many other [4].

- Structure, architecture, design: Within the manually constructed ontology the basic interest is considered here. For the purpose of meeting specific pre-defined principles or properties, the ontology needs auxiliary concerns within it. There is also a need for further enhancement which however needs a proper reason for it. There is a manual completion of this particular type of evaluation.

1.2 PHYLOGENY VISUALIZATION METHOD

There are two categorizations of the phylogentic methods are distance based method and character based method. The evolutionary information that is known is used for the character based methods. On the basis of the distance matrix, the cluster based computations are gathered. The steps involved here are:

a) Neighbor Joining Method: The distance based clustering method is referred to as the Neighboring Joining Method. The collection of each of the gathered species is evaluated and further, for the resulting tree, the sum of length of the branch is computed. As the nearest neighbor the smallest sum of the match of species is considered and is further combined. Amongst the two joined species a new branch is added. Further the remaining tree and the branch length are recomputed. Till there is any single terminal available, the procedure keeps rehashing.

b) UPGMA Method: The collection of two species that have least distance amongst them as per the distance matrix is known as the Unweighted Pair Group Method utilizing Arithmetic Average (UPGMA). The centre point of two species is referred to as a new hub. The distance from the new hub to the various nodes is the result of the arithmetic average [5].

c) Maximum Parsimony Method: The character based method that is utilized for handling the phylogeny relationships from the various organisms is known as the maximum parsimony method. The easiest explanation of data is proposed within this method as there is a need of very less substitutions within all sequences which further helps in deriving new systems from the normal ancestors existing.

d) Maximum Likelihood Method: A prevalent factual method that is utilized for fitting the measureable model to the data is known as maximum probability estimation (MLE). For the factual inferences, this method is mainly involved. For the purpose of identifying the tree topology that has highest probability a technique is utilized within the phylogeny method. The data as well as model of the grouping evolution are involved here. For the purpose of estimating the branch lengths and other various evolutionary parameters, this method is also utilized.

1.3 ONTOLOGY MODEL FOR PHYLOGENY VISUALIZATION

The framework of proposing work for visualizing phylogeny relationship using ontology approach is presented here. The proposed framework comprises of Phylogeny Creation, Ontology Design, and Visualization.

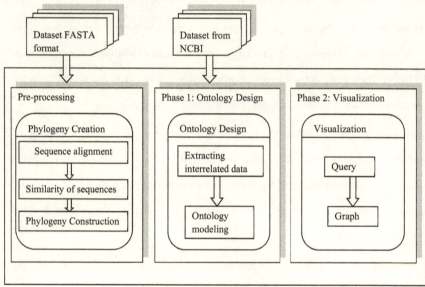

Fig 1.1 Ontology Model for Phylogeny Visualization

i. **Dataset:**

From NCBI the data set is utilized within the proposed work. For the phylogenetic tree construction, the FASTA sequence of hominidae family is extracted. The great primates and people are involved within the Hominidae. A taxonomic family of primates is framed within the hominidae frame which involves the following four categories:

6

1) Chimpanzee (pan)

2) Gorilla (gorilla)

3) Humans (homo) and

4) Orangutans (pongo).

The dataset contains FASTA sequence information of 12 organisms.

ii. **Phylogenetic Creation:**

The main phase of Phylogeny creation contains of three steps. They are Similarity of sequence, Sequence Alignment, and Phylogeny tree construction [6].

- **Similarities of sequences:** It is mainly the degree of sequence character amongst the 2 nucleotide sequences. The comparison of many of the sequences is required for aligning numerous of them. This helps in determining the evolutionary relationship amongst the various organisms present.

- **Sequence Alignment:** For the purpose of arranging the sequence of DNA, RNA and protein the sequence alignment method is utilized. The locale of similarity is identified here which might be a result of the basic, functional or the evolutionary relationship amongst the sequences. They are mainly utilized for the non-biological sequences.

- **Pairwise Distance:** For the purpose of calculating the pairwise distance, various distance algorithms are provided. At any given movement, the two aligned sequences are compared within the distance metrics. A matrix that has all provided sequence pairs is provided within this matrix. The changes of the quantity are counted within each comparison. In terms of the general sequence length all the changes are further presented. The pairwise distance is known as the final estimate of the distinction amongst each executed match of the sequences.

7

- **Multiple Sequence Alignment:** There are three biological sequences presented here for aligning the sequence in this process. There is a relationship present amongst the evolutionary relationships which provide the input set of the query sequences and are generated from the previous proposed methods only. The sequences of the shared evolutionary origins are also presented here along with an analysis of the phylogenetic methods.

- **Multiple Sequence Alignment:** A sequence alignment of minimum three biological sequences mainly DNA, RNA or protein is known as the multiple sequence alignment process. An evolutionary relationship is provided by the input set of query sequences according to which the lineage is shared. It is an extension of the already present process. Within the evolutionary origins, the sharing of sequences can be provided by acknowledging the sequence and analyzing the phylogenetic method [7].

iii. **Ontology Design phase**

There are two phases involved within the secondary phase known as the ontology design. They are extracting interrelated data and Ontology Modeling.

a. Extracting interrelated data: from the gene dataset, the interrelated data is extracted along with the details of the organisms presented within the phylogeny which include the gene information, and gene functional description within the gene ontology. With the help of ontology terminologies, the representation of this extracted data is done. Further, for designing the ontology model, the protégé tool is utilized.

b. Ontology Modeling: The part of the second phase is the ontology modeling method. The gene information is mapped here in which the schema is designed for mapping the gene information. The properties of Hominidae species are also represented here. Within the gene dataset, the

8

examination of the phase is done for mapping the attributed of gene within a class, and sub class. The object and data properties are mapped for establishing the entities within the class within this method.

- **Ontology Schema for Phylogeny:** The hominidae species is represented as base class in the ontology method. Here the class, object properties as well as data properties are present. There are three classes further present which are gene, Go_id and the gene functionality. For the purpose of mapping the two base classes, the object properties are utilized. Basically it involves the five different properties that are belongs_to, has_go, has_gene, has_evidence, and has_functionality.

  There are alternate classes such as GO_ID and Gene Functionality to which the class gene is mapped. There are various processes involved within the gene functionality such as the biological process, molecular function and the cellular components. For providing the information related to the gene for mapping the specific gene records, this method is designed. It provides the facilities with respect to the phylogeny view of the species.

Ontology Terminologies

There are various terms involved while representing the relationship of entities which are provided within the protégé tool as mentioned below [8].

➤ **Class**

- A named class or expression is represented by the equivalent classes within each passage which is basically equal to the present chosen class.
- A named class or expression is provided by each super class of the section. This is mainly the super class of the current chosen class.

- There are random super classes in which the protégé observes all the earlier selected classes and gathers the larger part of the random super class. This class is further displayed within this section.

- An individual is determined by the members of each section in this class for the purpose of assertion aphorism.

- A single disjoint statement is present by the disjoint classes within each section. There are two more classes involve within the disjoint statement.

➢ Object Properties contains in the following sections:

- The member of a class is presented within the domain of an individual in the subject of relation with the help of the available property. Providing an intersection, various entries are provided.

- If an object is in relation of an individual, the ranges are utilized that help in determining their relation which ensures that it is a member of the particular class.

- Each section is equal to the property of the equivalent object properties.

- Within the editor, the disjoint properties are to be multi-selected for making the disjoint set include in this property.

➢ **Individuals:** The individuals present within the ontology the value present within the each class. The ontology concepts are required for the identifying the attributes within the gene details [9].

iv. **Visualization**

The extraction of the functionality and relationships from the genes is done within the secondary phase. There are two parts in which it is categorized. They are the query and the graph visualization. For inferring the phylogeny of the organism that contains the interrelated data, the information from the generated ontology is retrieved within the query. The two parameters involved are the Class name and the object property name value "" which is also a syntax for recovering information on the basis of class and object property with value.

a. DL Query: With the help of DL Query tab within the tool, the information related to the genes is gathered. A string and easy-to-use feature is provided by the DL Query tab which involves the searching of a classified ontology. It provides a standard plug-in for the protégé 4 tool. On the basis of the Manchester OWL syntax, the query language is provided by the plug-in. it also has an easy to utilized syntax. The particular class, property or an individual is presented on the basis of complete information related to it that is gathered and presented in a frame.

b. Graph: A part of the protégé tool that provides graphical representation of the information related to the organisms is known as the graph perception. In involves various classes and their properties that are mapped t the selected class [10].

1.3.1 Phylogeny Pipeline

From the set of sequences, the phylogenetic tree is allowed to be worked by the pipeline within the core system. A succession of the Perl modules that wrap the distinctive external programming programs within this pipeline mainly requires three modes. Various other programs are also required here that are not mentioned here which are required for making the junction between the main programs, providing output to the results within various formats, and modifying the tree or rearranging it to provide various editions within it. these all methods proposed here provide certain parameters such that the methods can be executed in a beneficiary manner within the systems.

a. 'One Click' mode: The clients that do not want to manage the program and parameter selection are targeted within the 'one click' mode. The well identified programs such as

11

MUSCLE for multiple alignments, Gblocks for automatic alignment curation, PhyML for tree building and TreeDyn for tree drawing are already present within the pipeline for running and associating with them. As per the results it is examined that the programs are fast as well as accurate. With the help of various databases, the MUSCLE was assessed which involved BAliBASE benchmark. During the publication duration, the highest ranking of any of the methods was achieved here. The accuracy of PhyML was identified to be similar to that of the already existing phylogeny programs utilizing simulated data. Here, the magnitude of one request is however faster. There have been various enhancements proposed in both the programs. The _650 and _1000 citations in Web of Science is utilized in case of MUSCLE and PhyML, is utilized individually here. The properties of these systems have been stated to be as robust, stable and error free. There have been various clients who have reported it as very beneficial. There have been various considerable measures taken to assist the default options and parameter values. These values have been utilized in 'one click' mode and are suitable for various studies. For the purpose of testing the branch support, the PhyML runs along with the aLRT method. On the basis of the standard likelihood ratio test, the main examination is based. This process has higher speed as compared to the earlier bootstrap method in terms of providing computations. Similar trees are given as output in both the methods. There might be however, different branch supports along with their correlation. There is an increase in speed of the routine phylogenetic examinations on the basis of this mode. The request is required to be submitted and the set of sequences is required to be loaded by the clients here [11].

b. 'Advanced' mode: Similar to the pipeline utilized in the 'one click' mode, the pipeline is utilized in the advanced mode as well where the clients can modify the settings present within each of the program. The clients can choose the steps that are to be performed as per the flexibility. A set of uncommitted sequences where the alignment is a tree in Newick format is

12

present within the input data. There is various record formats supported as well. Within the each step, the results of the system are inspected before the execution of next program. This is done to detect the issues and rearrange te parameters by the clients within this process.

c. 'A la Carte' mode: The similar interface as the advanced mode is presented with the help of this mode. However, the effectiveness of running, testing and comparing of numerous programs are provided by this method. An easy to understanding pipeline is proposed through this mechanism in which the steps that are to be performed can be chosen by the clients along with the program that is to be utilized for them as individual. Various mechanisms are proposed here which help in providing the exactness and which provide their own functionalities which attain he structure information through which the alignments can be enhanced.

d. Tree visualization and drawing: The interpretation of an image of the tree is to be provided by any of the three modes present within the phylogenetic three reconstruction method. With the help of various TreeDyn options, the enhancing and drawing of the tree image is allowed with the help of phylogeny.fr. The options include the modification in shape of tree, font style, text and branches shade, and selection of root. Within the PNG and PDF formats, the image of the tree can be gained. For publication, it can be incorporate within any artwork in future [12].

1.4 INTRODUCTION TO DRUG DETECTION

On the basis of properties of quantum mechanics the simulating molecules are allowed to interact with each other within the structural bioinformatics tools. This has been developed with the advancements in the biomedical research area. The techniques developed have been a part of the drug design and drug discovery methods. The gathered information is used for identification, design and optimization of newly evolving drugs within this field. The discovery of a molecule that is ready to bind and activate or inhibit a molecular target which is mainly a protein, is done

13

in the drug search and discovery method. The lead components are those compounds that exceed certain threshold value as they can exceed the exceptions of a protein. The search proposed here is a very manual procedure followed. For the searching methods, the high-throughput screening (HTS) is the most commonly utilized technique that helps in searching within the lead compounds. The researchers are allowed to test a large number of molecules with the help of robots. However, it is expensive and needs large number of drugs and compounds for it. For the purpose of assisting drug design the discussed concerns are to be taken care of. The quantity of compounds that are tried are to be minimized for computing by the interactions amongst the molecules.

Through analogy with the HTS, the Virtual Screening process was selected for naming this type of search. There is a need to know both the three-dimensional structure of the target receptor as well as the testing compound in order to sort the simulations. The complete mechanism is known as Structure-based Virtual Screening (SBVS). Through the search of similar molecules to the compounds with known activity, a Ligand-based Virtual Screening (LBVS) method is used in case where the structure of the molecular target is not accessible. For the purpose of drug discovery considering it as a LBVS screening approach, the machine learning is a vital resource. There is less number of computational resources required as compared to the calculation of molecule interactions within these techniques. Due to the generalization capacity, the different hits are to be discovered as compared to the various similarity methods. A solid resurgence is provided by the AI as well as the other machine learning techniques. A quantitative and qualitative requirement is to be ensured within this area of research which is to be ensured b the deep learning (DL) as well as the other latest techniques within the neural networks. Within the bioinformatics and computational biology however, these methods have not achieved much involvement.

14

1.5 VIRTUAL SCREENING BACKGROUNG

As a benefit to the HTS testing, the computational drug search method can be utilized. The false negatives can be identified here along with the reduction of costs. Large numbers of VS strategies are limited higher as compared to the HTS which is further utilized for recognizing the sets of compounds along with the exceptional structural diversity. On the better simulations, the best candidates have been identified ever since. The advantages of using the computational methods as a part of the drug search, the advantages of various techniques have been discussed. VS is a knowledge-driven method within is different from the HTS approach and is type of random search within the library of compounds. The main highlight here is of the classification of VS methods. The specific non-exclusive methods can be used for addressing the virtual screening with the help of the structural information present. The screening methods involve the two different types of strategies. They are the structure-based VS and the ligand-based VS methods [13].

The 3D targeted structural information of requirement is handled with the help of structure-based VS (SBVS). There are various methods through which the target structure might be derived. There is a need to analyze a lot of problems when a biological target is to be considered for SBVS. Actually, the recognizable proof of ligand binding locales on biological targets is turning out to be progressively important. The requirement for novel modulators of protein/gene function has as of late guided established researchers to seek after druggable allosteric binding pockets. This is quite beneficial thus. Another consideration for SBVS incorporates the watchful decision of the compound library to be screened in the VS exercise as indicated by the target being referred to, and the preprocessing of libraries with a specific end goal to assign the correct stereochemistry, tautomeric, and protonation states [14].

In general, most authors classify their work in one of these three categories

1. Structure-based VS

2. Ligand-based VS

3. Combinatorial or structure-based de novo design

There is a need to name some procedures in a different category even when they are placed in one of the primary classes of the system. It is required to catalogue the below mentioned two classifications for few methods:

4. Chemogenomics

5. Machine Learning

1.5.1 Structure-Based Virtual Screening: There are many new targets that are to be highlighted with the modern sequencing technologies. A speculative calculation of the interaction of molecules with another can be done with the utilization of the structural information given. In both, the important and related research, the researchers have achieved better results. However, there are many challenges also being faced by them such as the flexibility of protein side is to be taken care of. All such requirements are to be considered further.

1.5.2 Ligand-Based Virtual Screening: A ligand focusing screening technique is to be applied when the 3D structure of the target is not accessible. For the purpose of retrieving various potentially active molecules on the basis o similarity measures, the information related to active

or non-active compounds is required. This whole concept is known to be the similarity search method. The definition of chemical similarity amongst the molecules is the main factor within this method. In relation to the molecular activity, the employed information must be related. A quick comparison amongst the various compounds is proposed through the description here. The

16

combination of ligand based and structure-based VS methods for leveraging huge range of accessible information is gaining popularity these days. The two hybridizing the methods classified here are the sequential scheme and the parallel scheme. The already present results have been outperformed with the help of new technology. The screening cannot the improved on purpose with the application of diverse methods collectively [15].

1.5.3 Combinatorial or de novo Design: The new compounds are synthesized by connecting various chemical elements with the help of various generated technologies. The large libraries of compounds that are to be screened are also built here. A new design here is the real leap forward related to the virtual screening. By guiding suggestions within the browsing area with the help of some combinational libraries that are constructed joining the previous searches, there is a huge space of chemical compounds generated. The best combination of molecular fragments can be identified that are present within the complete ligand. A more appropriate source of test compounds is selected by the libraries generated on these lines. As the structural diversity is appropriate, these methods are more popular. There are various compounds that have been made with the help of various approaches. There are two broader classifications for this which are atom-based and fragment-based. The molecule is created atom by atom within the atom-based methods. However, sets of predefined molecular building squares are utilized for fragment-based methods. There molecular building squares are related to the synthesis of method. The compounds are allowed to be gathered quickly in the second method as per the goal. However, there are very less particular designs delivered here.

1.5.4 Chemogenomics: Chemogenomics is a method that works similar to that of the screening strategy. Along with the compound classes and the protein families, the VS method works. The classic one-ligand and the one-protein view point are not utilized here. A new

17

viewpoint is presented here which shifts from focusing on receptors that are individual entities to the larger global viewpoint in real. Related to the functions, the structure of proteins is connected. There are many regular components within the receptors of the diverse groups or families. There is an assumption which states that similar receptors bind similar ligands. The compounds and ligands of same receptors are performed with the help of drug discovery of the chemogenomics. Also, the similar compounds to these ligands are provided within this method. The chemogenomics system requires setting up the similarity measures even when in a more general manner, which is same as that of the search methods analyzed. There can be a similar employment of the one-target methods within the similar measures [16].

1.5.5 Machine Learning and Virtual Screening: Within the VS category, the machine learning is the method that provides numerous computations for various orders of techniques. Here, for the purpose of exploiting the accessible information, the basic estimations are replaced with the canny models that are especially trained to do so. Towards both active and non-active compounds, the basic information is required. However, the advancement in knowledge will further help in enhancing the accuracy of results and providing variety in them. Amongst the most known applications of the supervised ML within the VS the creation of QSAR model is the best known models. An outstanding potential is seen in this method for the modeling of complex non-linear relationships within the executions. Within this area and the neural nets, the main thought shared is depicted by the artificial neural networks (ANN). Within the QSAR processing, for instance, the multilayer perceptron or probabilistic neural networks are connected in a proper manner. Due to the generalization capacity of support vector machines, there introduction became a great success further. In the search of new active compounds and various phases of the drug design, the primary alternative features of the system are applied. Within the

18

cheminformatics area, the other related calculations have been added. There has been a variant attention for the decision trees due to the generation of models that allow the translation of results related to the decision rules. There are the models utilized for the homogeneous methods that gather due to the extreme sensitivity as per the modifications made within the data. A comparative alternate for this technique is thus the Random Forest (RF) ensemble method. It is very important method amongst the SVM related techniques. Within the various supervised tasks such as the creation of QSAR relationships or the investigation of toxicity, there are various methods such as k-nearest neighbors and naïve bayes classifiers. They however, have less achievement as compared to other methods. Within various tasks, the unsupervised techniques and the enhanced methods have been linked. Within the toxic studies and design of the new compounds, the self-organizing maps (SOM) have proved to be better. For the purpose of combinatorial design, there are various search methods such as genetic calculations, ant colonies, and particle swarm optimization applied. They generate the QSAR relationships within these systems [17].

1.6 GRAPHICS PROCESSING UNIT (GPU)

A GPU is a particular device designed to rapidly manipulate high measures of graphical pixels. Historically, GPU were conceived for being used in advanced graphics and videogames. All the more as of late interfaces have been worked to interact with codes not identified with graphical purposes, for instance for linear algebraic controls. The involvement of GPU for providing basic reason logical and engineering computing is known as the general-reason GPU computing method. The utilization of CPU and GPU in a collective manner within a heterogeneous co-processing computing model is the basic concept of this method. On the CPU, the application runs in a sequence and there is an increase in speed of the computationally-intensive part within the GPU. For the purpose of lifting the performance of GPU in terms of its high-performance, the speed of the application is made to be higher in terms of the view of client. Anything that was earlier experienced or present within the PC is completely changed with the help of GPU. There is a need of higher processing speed due to the increase in involvement of 3D in day to day lives. There are computationally intensive transform and lighting calculations present within the CPU which are offloaded to the GPU as per the modifications made in GPU. This further helps in increasing the speed of processing within the systems. Without any compromises in the performance, the details and complexity of the network are enhanced. This enhancement in GPU thus provides very beneficial profit for nothing in return. The interaction of objects with each other and their neighbors is copied in a robust manner with the help of virtual representations of the issues. Each of the variables can be processed through the expected intense split-second computations. The CPU resources execute the higher functionalities of the process and there are no special processes of its own [18].

1.6.1 Background on GPU computing using CUDA

Within an extension of the C language the programmers can write the code utilizing the CUDA model. The code will keep running in a highly parallel manner on the GPU. It is very clear to the programmer regarding the details of the mapping of code on the physical processing units. Further, a parallel code can be written on the basis of this which can help in scaling the devices which have various parallel processing capabilities. A C function also known as kernel is utilized for running each code on the GPU. From the C/C++ code the function can be called which is being executed as a C function. The memory modules that can be physically separated from each other can be executed on the basis of CPU and GPU. A different memory space is required to be maintained on the memory space of GPU's separate device memory due to this. A memory region is pre-allocated at the initial stage of execution for fulfilling such requirement. A full event frame is made to be fit here on the particular device memory of the GPU when the execution is about to start. For the purpose of providing intermediate results and outputs related to the computation of kernel, extra space is allocated. As arguments the pointers are provided to the memory regions when there is a need to provide the kernel call. For providing an investigation of the complete event frame, the following steps are required [19]:

1. On the pre-allocated region of the GPU device memory, the contents of the event frame are copies by the worker thread in the beginning.

2. The kernel function of an accessible checker algorithm is called through this. In a parallel and asynchronous manner with the CPU, the kernel function is executed by the GPU cores. During the calling of the kernel function, the arguments of the pointed to the device memory region are passed. Here the current frame is stored along with the additional values such as the quantity of events present within the frame. On the multiple cores and threads, each kernel is executed in single instruction, multiple data (SIMD) manner.

3. In order to process further, the CUDA routines are utilized which help in synchronizing the execution of kernel. The result of the checking is copied by the worker thread when there is unlimited supply of the kernel call. There are various pairs of accessed during the data-race detection from GPU's device memory to the CPU's memory which are to be reported after the processing.

The parallel kernels for ERASER and GOLDILOCKS algorithm are introduced for removing the challenges faced by the existing methods. The challenges provided with huge number of cores that are accessible on the GPU, the test within the writing kernels are exchanges.

1.6.2 KUDA approach

The overhead of the customary method is minimized with the help of division of monitoring and analyzing of CPU and GPU together. Here, both of the tasks are executed on the similar threads or cores. The speed of program and the examination code is similar. Once the program terminates, the code also ends soon after that. The implementation of a prototype tool known as KUDA is done here. The KUDA is linked with the collection of multithreaded benchmarks. There are two parts in which the KUDA algorithm is divided [20]:

1. The first part involves the core functionality which includes the routines in which the events are recorded, the event frames are manages and the execution of race detection kernels on the GPU, all within the dynamic library. The kernels can be written and called with the help of CUDA 4.0 library which will help in analyzing frames. Also, the GPU resources can be managed through this process. Global memory is utilized for executing the experiments, however, the constant and texture memory can also be utilized within this method. The constant and texture memory are utilized for the utilization in the manner of the working of event frames with the help of kernel. The fast readonly access holds such frames within its cache.

2. The x86 binaries are to be dynamically instrumented with the help of Pin tool. The main objective here is to callback the routines within the dynamic library in respect of specific events. The multithreaded programs that are created with the help of pthreads library are supported by the Pin tool. Various actions are performed through this tool such as the creation, joining, and synchronization of various threads.

CHAPTER 2
LITERATURE REVIEW

Vatanjeet Singh et al. [21] presented an ultra wide band (UWB) method which is a multi resonant optical antenna is proposed in this paper which involves the FR4 dielectric constant 4.4 within it . Within this proposed antenna design the gap coupled feeding system is also involved. There is copper material utilized within the ground, fix as well as the feed line of the system. There are numerous resonant frequencies present within the required return loss that are present within the design of this proposed method. There has been a particular range described for this system as well. In terms of various parameters such as return loss, directivity, gain and many others, the performance of optical antenna has been calculated. In case of providing higher reverberating frequencies, there is a need to design higher gain and directivity within this novel design. Within various applications the novel antenna can be implemented such that the various enhancements can be seen. It has been analyzed that gain and directivity has high magnitude at high resonant frequencies. It has additionally been watched that the proposed antenna has greatest gain of 7.94dB at resonant frequency 7.73 THz and has the most extreme directivity of 11.70dBi at resonant frequency 7.73 THz. The proposed antenna covers diverse range of applications, for example, detection of explosives, drugs (cocaine, heroin), colon cancer, mind tumor and security applications, for example, mail screening examination and monitoring water content in leaves.

Nima Aliakbarinodehi et al. [22] proposed on the nano-structure biosensors with respect of the electro-active cancer-drug identification. The enhancement of level of sensitivity and the limit of detection of the two different nano-structured biosensors is focused in this paper. This is done mainly to discover the best decision that will provide the exact calculation of the quantity of

23

etoposide present. Etoposide is basically a largely used elctroacitve cancer drug which is to be utilized at limited concentration. There have been various amount of etoposide concentration detected within certain applications. There have been various limits set as per the utilization of this drug and the amount of drugs detected have been recorded as per the application within the systems involving multi-walled carbon nano-tube and gold nano-particle based electrodes. There has been a record of the drugs gathered from other various electrodes and nano-tubes as well. The GNP-SPE method has been proposed in this paper for providing higher sensitivity and the required functionality along with less LOD. This is required for detecting the electro-active drugs within the etoposide. There are numerous other factors as well that effect the impact of dimensions of nano-particles on the performance and the material science involved here. This is the main highlight of the future studies to be presented ahead.

Patricia Vazquezet al. [23] provide in a hollow microneedle, the integration of an electrochemical miniaturized scale. The recognition of the concentration of drugs present within the fluids of body is the main objective of this new sensor platform being derived in this paper. There have although been large number of scenarios in which the immiscible liquid interfaces have been involved in the field of electrochemistry. However, the involvement of microneedle within this integration has been the first one. Without extracting any physiological fluid within these systems, the drugs can be detected which is a major advantage of this technology. This is not possible within the other existing approaches as there is a need to recognize ionic species that is against the redox processes. Within the physiological buffer, the detection of microneedle platform is done. It is seen through the various calibrations provided for the sensitivity of the systems; the various experiments have been conducted. These results are also compared with the already existing highly-sensitive techniques. With the help of artificial saliva that has higher sensitivity, the detection of propranolol was done with the help of array of sensors. There is a need of high sensitivity and a limit required for detecting the necessity of the systems. As per the simulation results achieved, there have been depicted huge enhancements in the results and these enhancements have resulted in enhancing the systems on the basis of various aspects.

Pedro R. Gomes et al. [24] concern is to provide a controlled drug administration for the patients that are suffering from a particular type of disease known as Brugada Syndrome (BS). Under the proper electrocardiogram (ECG) monitoring, there are various types of drugs that are provided under proper surveillance and the quantity provided is also monitored. In case when there is some ECG related un-stabilized condition occurring within the system it is to be identified and stopped to avoid any mis-happenings. With the involvement of Hidden Markov Models (HMM) that is basically a pattern recognition technique; the abnormalities present within the system can be identified. There are various features that extracted from the three scales of the Wavelet Transform (WT) method. Compared to the classification of typical and abnormal pulses, the performance of these systems has provided systems with an efficiency of 98%. From the standard MIT-BIH arrhythmia database, there is a proper training provided for the systems. The low content frequency is provided by the P-wave method and the higher content frequency is provided by the QRS systems. There have been various enhancements proposed within the paper that have increased the efficiency of the existing mechanisms and the methods have been involved within the trending applications to provide accurate results. The results are compared with the results achieved from existing approaches also.

Daniela De Venuto et al. [25] proposed an electrochemical biosensor for the molecules that are involved within the personalized machine. These systems have pH and temperature shift monitoring systems within them. The extensive majority of the drugs is done by the electrochemical sensors that are on the basis of cytochromes P450. Within the pharamacological treatments, these sensors are utilized. Within the various electrochemical interface systems, the various drugs are detected with the help of similar cytochrome. The type of drug is differentiated by the potential systems and the concerned systems also provide the amount of drug concentrated there. There might be various pH differences on the basis of which the conditions of patients can be identified. In this paper, an example of variations is proposed in this paper along with a new design that might help in multiplexing the biosensing across various pH and temperature control systems. for the need of monitoring the personal therapies of the patients, the systems proposed and designed within this paper are ensured to be reliable and robust so that they prove to be beneficial to the current applications.

S. Sara Ghoreishizadeh et al. [26] involved new technologies within the various drug treatment methods, that can monitor the concentration of drug within the blood of the patient. Within this paper, an anti-cancer drug known as Etoposide has been selected as model for cyclic voltammetry drug identifications. The sensitivity of the system is enhanced with the involvement of carbon nanotubes that are the electron-exchange mediators. For the need of providing cyclic voltammograms, a low frequency and slope triangular-wave method is proposed. For correctly determining the amount of drug present within the body of patient, the cyclic voltammograms have been very efficient. The real time implementation of VLSI which is completely integration within the cyclic voltammetry estimations is required within this paper. There is a need to basically reduce the cost of the chip that is utilized for detection and monitoring the drug. With the help of Direct Digital Synthesis (DDS) method, a triangular wave generator CMOS circuit is proposed in this paper. At 0.18 μm, the implementation of circuit is done which proposed the chance of converting the slope of triangular voltage within a wide range. There are both analog as well as digital parts involved that analyze the power consumption of the whole circuit. The devices that are completely implantable and remotely powered within certain applications are to be considered here as there is very less power consumption within such services. There will be a fabrication of current readout circuit on a chip for providing drug detection that is based on the CV mechanism.

M. Koutalonis et al. [27] with the help of the postal and dispatch administrations, the drugs are pirated within a nation. For the purpose of avoiding such actions, there is a need to check the exchanging parcels across the nations and to do so there is a need to develop higher level of security systems. For the end clients of a system there is a need of providing false, positive and negative results. The packets that contain drugs are not to be lost and also the packets that do not have any drugs should not provide hindrance in the workflow. For the need of meeting certain requirement, the previous studies are examined and the x-beam diffraction method has been chosen for this purpose as it has shown very positive results in identifying the drugs as compared to the various other technologies. Due to the crystalline pattern of the drugs and the unique diffraction signature, this method has been selected. As there are very effective results achieved, there have been many evolvements that have been made by keeping in base of this technology. Within this paper, by simulating the energy dispersive x-beam diffraction from the powder diffraction profiles of a few materials a new simulation model is proposed. There has been a collection of the thousands of materials within a database. The checking of some infield systems for identifying the drug is the main aim of this study. The optimum that is produced within this method is settled here. This systems has provided improvement in the results.

R.Sindhu et al. [28] Due to the expansion of GenBank database, the biologists have put forth the information that is similar to this context. By studying the merits and demerits of the DNAs of the daily lives of various individuals, the reconstruction of branches is to be done with the help of researchers. The study of the historical patterns of relationships amongst various organisms that has evolved from the actions of evolutionary process is known as the phylogeny process. With the help of branching cladograms and phylogenetic tree diagrams, the phylogenetic relationships have been shown. Within the fields of bioinformatics and data mining, the mining of biological data has been a very effective trend that is being followed. For the need of interrupting the information related to the sequences, the data mining methods have been included in biology. For the need of providing revelation within the data distribution and patterns present within the data, the clustering mechanism is to be involved. For the need of locating the evolutionary relationship with the help of data mining, a hierarchical agglomerative clustering system is presented within this research study.

Go-Ebi et al. [29] has viewed that there are special spaces filled by the Genet Ontology (GO) method within the fields of molecular as well cellular biology. This is due to the organized and controlled vocabularies they provide as well as the classifications present. Within the applications of genes, gene items as well as sequences, this method has gained huge popularity. The GO method is utilized by numerous model organism databases and genome annotation groups. Towards the GO asset, the annotation sets belong. The vocabularies and contributed annotations are integrated with the help of GO database. Within numerous formats, the information is provided with complete access with the help of this application. For the need of expanding the GO vocabularies, the GO consortium is providing enhancements with the help of various experts. The extensive documentation within the GO project is provided with complete access with the help of the GO web applications. The applications that use GO data for the purpose of examining functional criteria are linked with the help of this application. The community development related to the bioinformatics standards is provided with the help of the ongoing case of GO project.

Naruya Saitou et al. [30] proposed another method for the reconstruction of phylogenetic trees, method known as the neighbor-joining method. This is to be done from the evolutionary distance data. The pairs of operational taxonomic units are to be identified which will further reduce the length of aggregate branch at each stage of clustering. This is the main objective of this proposed method. Further, it can also provide the branch lengths and the topology of the niggardly tree. The appropriate unrooted tree is also to be chosen by comparing with the other five tree-making technologies. The efficiency of the approaches is tested and the results are provided. As per the various experiments conducted, the neighbor-joining method as well as the Sattath and Tversky's methods are better in terms of various aspects within various applications. Similar to the Fitch and Margoliash method, the estimation of branch lengths is done here as well. There might also be achieved some negative branch lengths within the results. For disposing such negative values, there are two methods proposed as well. The first one is to provide a condition such that all the branches present within the tree should have positive values. The reestimation of the branch lengths is also to be done here. The second is to estimate that the reason behind the presence of negative values is the sampling error. It is also assumed that the values are not negative and are considered to be zero. Each negative value present within the brach of the tree is converted into zero here. As considered by the event that the absolute values of negative assumptions are always less, the secondary method is justifiable.

David Bryant et al. [31] used neighbor-net, a distance based method for constructing the phylogenetic networks. This method is based on the Neighbor-Joining (NJ) calculation of Saitou and Nei. A snapshot of the data is provided by this method in which there can be provided a more detail analysis related to this method. There is a proper scaling within the Neighbor-Net scales method which is not seen in the split decomposition method. There is a detailed and informative network produced for few hundred taxa here. There are three published data sets that are to be

29

analyzed within this paper for analyzing the performance of the proposed application with respect to various applications. These all the data sets provide a base for the demonstration of a base for the conversion of gene. As a component for the SplitTree4 software package is utilized within the application of Neighbor-Net. The initial step towards the complete reconstruction for the recombination histories is present within the splits graph. There is a treelike evolutionary history of the each gene or pair of contiguous segments present within the standard evolutionary model. The composition of the various histories is present within this system. The proposed method has provided a very strong initial step in this paper.

A.Dereeper et al. [32] presented three modes within the Phylogeny.fr method. The non-specialists are targeted within the 'A single click' mode and the ready-to-utilize pipeline is provided by it. This helps in increasing the speed at which the programs are executed along with the maintenance of accuracy and speed. There are various methods utilized here. They are MUSCLE that is used for multiple arrangements, PhyML that is utilized for tree building, and TreeDyn mainly used for tree rendering. For providing facilities to almost all the studies, these methods have been proposed which have all the variations for executing various methods. The input sequence is provided here by the user and further a ready-to-print tree is achieved. A same pipeline is proposed by the 'propelled' mode for each program that is to be customized by the various users. There is huge flexibility offered by the individually mode along with the sophistication. A different pipeline can be fabricated by selecting and setting up the needed steps. There are various tools selected here for providing various needs. By running he BLAST within the normal or concentrated databases, the preceding phylogenetic analysis is utilized in which users can gather the query sequence of neighbors through this approach. The neighbor sequences can be used as input for the phylogeny pipeline within the guide tree. The new features can be expanded within the modular architecture of the phylogeny.fr pipeline. There are new programs proposed as per the evolution of the field.

Scott V. Edwards et al. [33] focused on the determination of gene trees of the phylogenetic models. The species of phylogenies in which the gene trees are inserted are important here however. A Bayesian model is presented for estimating the species trees that record the variations present within the stochastic methods. These methods are to be present within the gene trees from the numerous unlinked loci that are sampled from the single species history within the coalescent process. There is a huge reduction in the obscure species tree in which the gene trees are sampled. The set of gene trees are recouped and the application of model to a 106-gene data set is demonstrated here. As compared to the existing methods, the proposed method has provided much positive outcomes. The yeast species tree that is within the congruent mode can be analyzed with the concatenated gene tree. Within the link method, a huge portion of the concatenated gene tree is required in these systems. it is demonstrated within the various simulations that using large number of loci, there can be an estimation provided for the highly resolved species trees. Here, the misleading of phylogeny can be done with the connection of the sequence data. In case when the proportion of gene trees that match the species is <10%, these methods are experimented. There can be only a few loci resolved in the case where the congruence of gene species is higher. For the purpose of combining data within the phylogenomics, the outputs of the system provide an alternative paradigm. The singularity of species histories is required here and there have been various studies proposed for the individual gene histories as well.

Gregory E. Jordan et al. [34] for visualizing and manipulating the phylogenetic tree data, the web-based tool known as PhyloWidgetis utilized. It is accessible through the internet or can also be downloaded as an individual application. The linking and customization of the PhyloWidget with the databases is done with the help of a simple URL-based API. This helps in providing a view of trees in perspective of their size. The customization of PhyloWidget is also ensured here. There is a need of various means for providing appropriate databases or applications within the program. Within the simple XML file, the toolbar, tool palette as well as the context menu are defined together. There is no addition of any tools or actions that are not required. Fom the default values, various parameters are transformed. The source code is either altered, the Javascript is utilized for changing the setting within the real-time and the parameters are used within the simple URL-based API that is arranged. A customized view is present within the databases that are an objective of the third option. Within the Newick, NHX and NEXUS formats, the PhyloWidget and can output trees within these methods. There are various formats of the picture such as JPEG, PNG or PDF file. The completely vector as well as content based output is provided by PDF. The publication-quality figures or for high-resolution printing is to be made ideal.

Fabio Pardi et al. [35] on the basis of the lattice of pairwise distances between taxa, there are various methods proposed related to the phylogenetic inference. The main objective here is to build a new tree that has branch length such that the leaves of the tree re vary close to each other. It is to be taken care that the distance amongst the leaves is very less and can be provided as input distances. The communication of optimal clues of branch lengths can be done with the help of easy combinatorial formulae within the event that holds the structure of the tree in a fixed manner. In this paper, the regular shape of the formula is presented along with the depiction of various properties. The combination of the formulae along with the normal tree reconstruction methods is the initial property. It provides the right tree as outcome when required data is provided to it. Secondary is the calculation of the branch lengths of the easy rearrangements of a tree. This is done in a quadratic time within the area of the three. This provides a way for allowing the appropriate application to utilized it relating to the hill climbing heuristics. The earlier proposed study of Mihaescu and Pachter in the field of branch length estimation is extended within this paper. The main highlight here is the tree and it works as a base for the new algorithms for reconstructing the trees at various distances.

Georgios A. Pavlopoulos et al. [36] generated huge amount of data from the various techniques like the ChIP-Chip, large-scale OMICS-approaches, genomics, proteomics and transcriptomics. There all mentioned technologies are basically the high-throughput technologies and so the data generation is large here. There is a need of less expensive and less demanding mechanism within the sequencing technologies. There is an involvement of large number of species within the huge evolutionary studies. This is a very challenging task as there are so many species present within it. Even there are various databases involved that store the data related to all those species. However the expansion of databases is also required as the data is not limited. Towards the connection of huge amounts of data the clustering analysis approach is utilized. The results of these algorithms are not visualized properly and so this method is to be experimented. The data within the databases is presented in 2D form and the huge part of the accessible visualization tools is displayed within such hierarchies. The requirement of utilization and interactivity is missed out within these systems. The straightforward large scale trees cannot be seen for example within the existing phylogenetic tree visualization tools. It only involves approximately thousands of hubs. Those tools presented within this study are basically the ones that visualize the biological trees and analysis. There have been various developments made within this paper. A uniform and standard computer readable format is represented within the tree hierarchies in this paper. The functionality and limitations of these tools is also stated. There is a need to develop many other new tools that is also proposed here along with the integration of various

33

data sources. The freely accessible software is present that provides the users various tree-representation methods that further help in providing the data analysis within the biology applications.

John P. Huelsenbeck [37] derieved various data divisions or subsets within various stochastic evolutionary models are provided within the MrBayes 3 that executes the Bayesian phylogenetic analysis. The various heterogeneous data sets that are present within the system such as the morphological, nucleotide, and protein are to be broken down through this method. a huge variety of the structured models that are present within the partition-based as well as shared parameters are put forth in this paper. The MPI works for parallelizing Metropolis coupling on the Macintosh or UNIX clusters within this program. In the existing approaches, there is very less information passed amongst the various chains. However, within the metropolis coupling, the parallel implementations are quite helpful. Here, the chains are distributed amongst the various processors. There is a precompiled version of the MacOS and windows platform provided within this site. The source code also adds on within the UNIX machine to provide services. There are various machines that are involved within this process. The POOCH mechanism is to be involved in each of this process within the parallel Macintosh version.

Satya S. Sahoo [38] provide supporting of information related to the semantic web technologies. The semantic gatherings and combinations are required for making it easy to run this method. For the purpose of understanding the genetic base of dependence factor of nicotine a system is proposed here. The gene as well as the pathway information is integrated here and the three complex biological queries are answered with the help of the integration of base knowledge. With the help of data involved from the pathway resources, the integrated method is populated. This is publically accessible within the BioPAX-perfect configuration as well as the gene resources for which the population procedure is generated. For the need of formulating the queries across the integrated knowledge base for answering the three biological queries, the SPARQL query language is used. The queries are formulated across the integrated knowledge to provide base for providing answer to the three biological queries. The hub genes are required to differentiate the simple SPARQL. These are those genes that provide an interest within the various pathways or also connect with the various other gene items. There is more problem when the genes that are identified as communicating within the mind. As there is no absence of a typical recognition related to the proteins, this method is proposed. Within the life sciences, the information integration is provided to the semantic web technologies that provide a proper framework. For providing integration to the huge volumes of data, the ontology-based integration is proposed that provides adaptable, manageable and extensible solution. For providing compensation to the heterogeneity across the namespaces, there are various resources that generate the mappings amongst various sources.

Ziheng Yang [39] presented various ranges of the data analysis for the prerequisite of equal branch lengths. This also involves larger branches and there are also many species present within all such categorizations. It is neither important nor a sufficient prerequisite for the method to provide less evolutions. There were various problems identified within the cmTent statistical estimation method for tree reconstruction. The proposed Felsenstein approach was proposed here for estimating the topology of the network. It also further helped in providing variations and extension that are different from the maximum likelihood estimation at the statistical parameter is proposed. It is seen through the application of Felsentein method that there is no sharing of the asymptotic efficiency of the maximum likelihood estimator of the statistical parameters within this system. For the purpose of studying the probability of MP to recover the tree the various simulations are performed. This is done within the hierarchy models of nucleotide substitution.

35

The executions results relative to the likelihood method are highlighted within this paper. All these simulations results have shown that the proposed mechanism has proved to be better in terms of the above mentioned parameters. The comparisons made are to be analyzed and the method is made to run under various applications for this.

M. Sharmila et al. [40] seen that the branch of biological science and IT that manages the study of various techniques that exclude, recover and investigate the biological data is known as bioinformatics. The study related to the living and non-living organisms that provide the historical patterns which further provides relationships with various organisms is known as phylogeny. On the basis of phylogeny visualization based representation, the ontology method is proposed in this paper. A superior visualization method is proposed here along with the interrelated data of the organisms. This data is represented within the phylogenetic tree. With the help of query and dynamic visualization methods, the data related to the organism can be gathered. There are various comparisons made amongst the proposed method and the existing ontology based visualization method. the view of the clustered phylogeny of organisms is presented within the proposed phylogenetic visualization method. There is no relative data of the organism present in it. It is seen within the proposed approach that the proposed method of picturing phylogeny gathers the information of organism from the phylogenetic tree available.

CHAPTER 3
PRESENT WORK

3.1 PROBLEM FORMULATION

The techniques has been discussed which is based on drug discovery. To discover new drugs the database of the drugs are scanned in the computational manner. The various algorithms have been proposed for the scanning of the database. To drive new values from the past database values techniques of screening tests are applied which is called virtual screening. To discover new drug various biological structures has been derived on the basic of some parameters of the already existing algorithms. The existing algorithm of discovering new drug has become major issue of pharmaceutical industries due to large number of resources used and discovery time is quite high. The parallel architecture CUDA provides the best solution for the drug discovery in terms of accuracy and execution time. In this work, improvement in the CUDA architecture will be proposed to increase performance by applied neural networks back propagation algorithm.

3.2 OBJECTIVES

1. To analyze various computational algorithm for virtual screening
2. To propose enhancement in CUDA and GP-CGC architecture for drug discovery
3. To compare the results in terms of different efficiency parameter.

3.3 RESEARCH METHODOLOGY

GPU becomes a highly parallel processor for the purpose of heavy workloads due to its ease of being programmed by Compute Unified Device Architecture (CUDA). GPU is an array which contains number of streaming processors (SPs). It also includes Single Instruction Multiple

Threads multiprocessors. Memory spaces are also available in the GPU which is helpful to microprocessors. All the multiprocessors can use the device memory which is also called the global memory. Its speed is however moderate but the size of this memory is the largest. The shared memory is the memory space of each multiprocessor which works very fast as compared to the global memory. The local memory is available per SP. A thread is known as the basic execution unit of a CUDA programming model. The GPU architecture is based to discovery new patterns for the drug discovery. To increase the accuracy of drug discovery technique c-mean clustering is applied with the SVM classifier. **Support vector machines**

A Support Vector Machine (SVM) is a discriminative classifier. It is formally defined by a separating hyperplane. The steps are explained below:

1. **Set up the training data:** The training data of this exercise is formed by a set of labeled 2D-points that belong to one of two different classes; one of the classes consists of one point and the other of three points.

2. **Set up SVM's parameters:** In this tutorial we have introduced the theory of SVMs in the simplest case, when the training examples are spread into two classes that are linearly separable. However, SVMs can be used in a wide variety of problems (e.g. problems with non-linearly separable data, a SVM using a kernel function to raise the dimensionality of the examples, etc). As a effect of this, we have to define some parameters before training the SVM. These parameters are stored in an object of the class CvSVMParams .

3. **Train the SVM:** We call the method CvSVM::train to build the SVM model [18]

4. **Regions classified by the SVM:** The method CvSVM::predict is used to classify an input sample using a trained SVM. In this example we have used this method in order to color the space depending on the prediction done by the SVM. In other words, an image is

traversed by interpreting its pixels as points of the Cartesian plane. Each of the points is colored depending on the class predicted by the SVM; in green if it is the class with label 1 and in blue if it is the class with label -1.

5. **Support vectors:** We use here a couple of methods to obtain information about the support vectors. The method CvSVM::get_support_vector_count outputs the total number of support vectors used in the problem and with the method CvSVM::get_support_vector we obtain each of the support vectors using an index. We have used these methods here to find the training examples that are support vectors and highlight them.

3.4 PSEUDO CODE OF PROPPOSED ALGORITHM

Step 1: Input the training and test data for the drug classification

Step 2: Repeat while loop for clustering

Step 2.1: Start for loop to input training set data

Step 2.1.1 : Apply c-mean technique to clustering of the data

End for

End While

Step 3: Repeat while unless all the data get classified

Step 3.1 : Match the training data and test data features using SVM classifier

Step 3.2 : Classify most similar and dissimilar data

End while

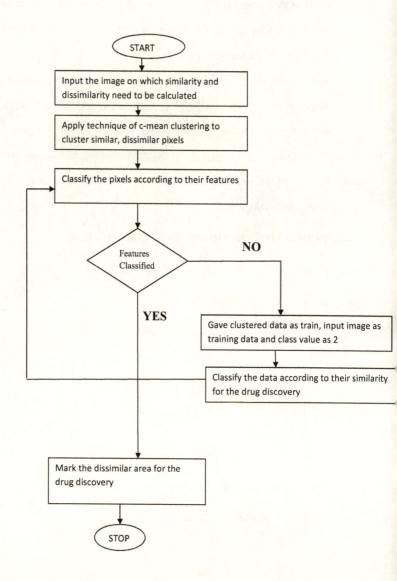

CHAPTER 4
RESULT AND DISCUSSION

This chapter presents the result computed using the current technique SVM and compare the results with other existing approaches.

4.1 RESULTS OBTAINED

Fig 4.1: Interface for the implementation

As shown in the figure 4.1, the interface is designed for the implementation of the drug discovery algorithm. In the interface the drug discovery button is defined which can process the algorithm and parameter value calculate the parameter PSNR, RMSE , accuracy and time

41

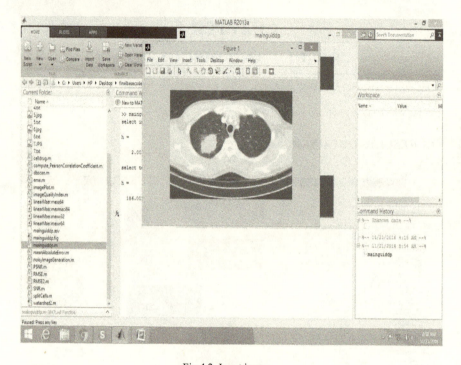

Fig 4.2: Input image

As shown in the figure 4.2, the interface which is designed for the implementation, drug discovery button is clicked and selected the image for discovery which is shown on the figure

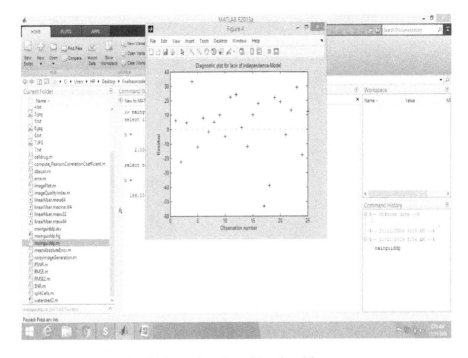

Fig 4.3: Observation values of the selected image

As shown in figure 4.3, the image which is given as input and that image which is selected on the

that image values which are similar is shown on the 2-D plane

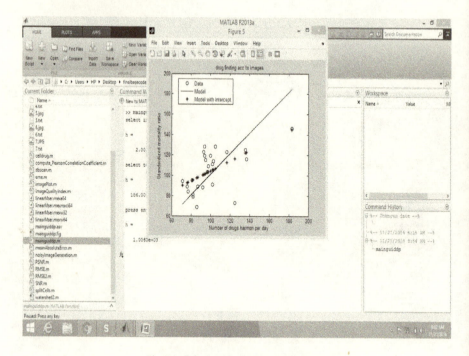

Fig 4.4: Calculate similarity of the data

As shown in figure 4.4, the images which are given as input on that image similarity value is calculated. The values of the similarity is plotted on the 2-D plane

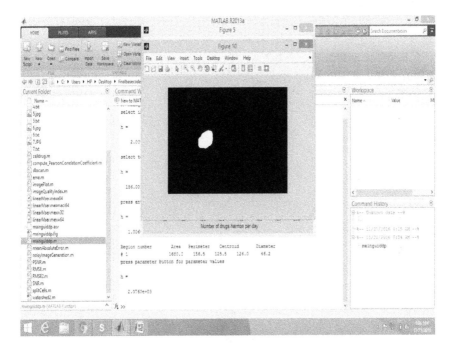

Fig 4.5: Erodded image

As shown in the figure 4.5, the image which is given as input on that image similarity index calculated. The image is erordded and image is marked with the white portion from where drug need to be discovered

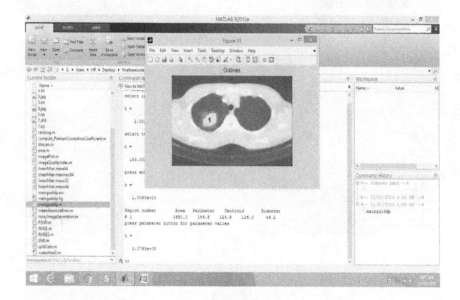

Fig 4.6: Portion marked

As shown in the figure 4.6, the image which is given as input on that image similarity index is calculated and portion from where drug need to be discovered is marked with number 1.

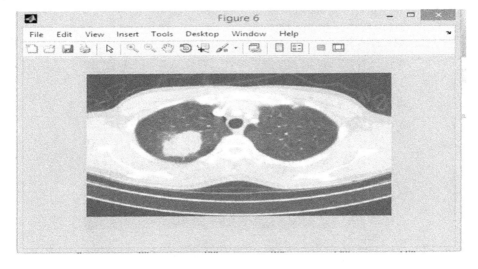

Fig 4.7: Input image for proposed technique

As shown in the figure 4.7, the image is taken as input which is used for the drug discovery. The technique of c-mean clustering is applied with the SVM classifier for the area classification

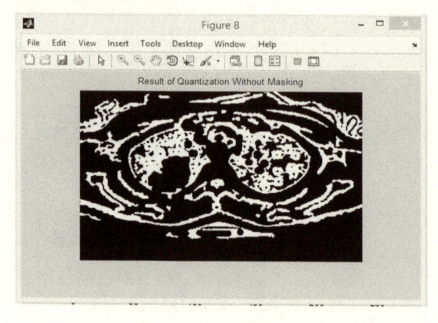

Fig 4.8: Apply technique of clustering

As shown in the figure 4.8, the technique of segmentation is applied which will segment the similar and dissimilar pixels of the input image. The spilt and merge technique is applied for the image segmentation

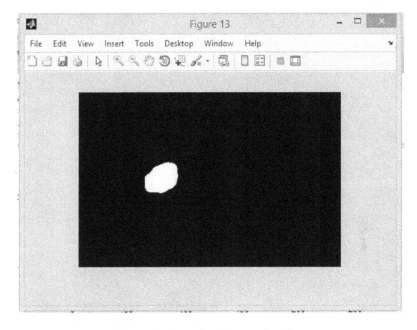

Fig 4.9: Apply of C-mean clustering

As shown in the figure 4.9, the technique of c-mean clustering is applied which will cluster the similar and dissimilar pixels from the image. The image pixels which are dissimilar are marked with the white color in the input image

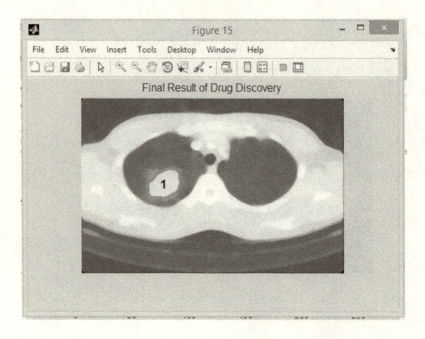

Fig 4.10: Final output

As shown in the figure 4.10, the image which is taken as input is processed and also the text file is taken as input for the final drug discovery. The technique of classification is applied which is mark the final area for which drug need to be discovered .

Table 4.1: PSNR Comparison

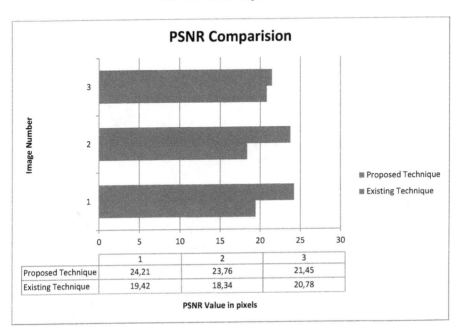

Table 4.1: PSNR Comparison

As shown in the table 4.1, The PSNR comparison of proposed and existing algorithm is done. It is been analyzed that PSNR of the proposed algorithm is more as compared to existing due to the use of classification technique.

Table 4.2: Accuracy Comparison

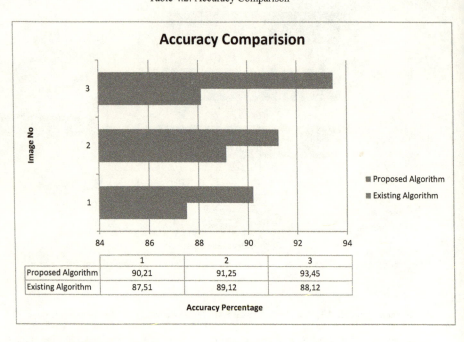

As shown in the table 4.2, The accuracy of the proposed and existing technique is compared and it is been analyzed that due to use of classification technique accuracy is increased at steady rate

CHAPTER 5
CONCLUSION AND FUTURE SCOPE

5.1 CONCLUSION

A GPU is a particular device designed to rapidly manipulate high measures of graphical pixels. Historically, GPU were conceived for being used in advanced graphics and videogames. All the more as of late interfaces have been worked to interact with codes not identified with graphical purposes, for instance for linear algebraic controls. The involvement of GPU for providing basic reason logical and engineering computing is known as the general-reason GPU computing method. The utilization of CPU and GPU in a collective manner within a heterogeneous co-processing computing model is the basic concept of this method. On the CPU, the application runs in a sequence and there is an increase in speed of the computationally-intensive part within the GPU. For the purpose of lifting the performance of GPU in terms of its high-performance, the speed of the application is made to be higher in terms of the view of client. Anything that was earlier experienced or present within the PC is completely changed with the help of GPU. There is a need of higher processing speed due to the increase in involvement of 3D in day to day lives. The code will keep running in a highly parallel manner on the GPU. It is very clear to the programmer regarding the details of the mapping of code on the physical processing units. Further, a parallel code can be written on the basis of this which can help in scaling the devices which have various parallel processing capabilities. A C function also known as kernel is utilized for running each code on the GPU. From the C/C++ code the function can be called which is being executed as a C function. The memory modules that can be physically separated from each other can be executed on the basis of CPU and GPU. In this work, it is been concluded that classification technique is applied which will classify the area for which disease need to discovered. The proposed technique is implemented in MATLAB and analyzed that accuracy is increased and execution time is reduced.

5.2 FUTURE SCOPE

Following are the various future prospective of this research work

1. The proposed technique can be compared with other techniques of drug discovery and test proposed algorithm in terms of various parameters

2. The proposed algorithm can be tested further by changing classification technique like decision tree, naïve bays etc

REFERENCES

[1] Markus Lill," Virtual Screening in Drug Design", 2013, In Silico Models for Drug Discovery, Methods in Molecular Biology, vol. 993

[2] Tiejun Cheng, Qingliang Li, Zhigang Zhou, Yanli Wang, and Stephen H. Bryant," Structure-Based Virtual Screening for Drug Discovery: a Problem-Centric Review", 2012, the AAPS Journal, Vol. 14, No. 1

[3] Ajinkya Nikam, Akshay Nara, Deepak Paliwal", Acceleration of Drug Discovery Process on GPU", 2015, IEEE, 978-1-4673-7910-6

[4] Javier Pérez-Sianes, Horacio Pérez-Sánchez and Fernando Díaz," Virtual Screening: A Challenge for Deep Learning", 2016, 10th International Conference on PACBB, vol34, issue 979

[5] Ja-Yu Lu, Li-Jin Chen, Tzeng-Fu Kao, Hsu-Hao Chang, and Chi-Kuang Sun", Terahertz Biochip for Illicit Drug Detection", 2006, IEEE, 1-55752-813-6

[6] Y. Sasaki, H. Hoshina, M. Yamashita, G. Okazaki, C. Otani, and K. Kawase," Detection and inspection device of illicit drugs in sealed envelopes using THz waves", 2007, IEEE, 239473-34927-27584

[7] Joe Miller, William S. Wilson, Wee Kuan Kek, Clive G. Wilson, and Deepak Uttamchandani," Drug Detection in the Living Eye Using a Novel, Minimally Invasive Optoelectronic System", 2003, IEEE SENSORS JOURNAL, Vol. 3, No. 1

[8] Narbik Manukian, Gregg D. Wilensky, John L. Kirkwood, Jung-Chou Chang," Neural Network Assisted Drug Detection in X-ray Images", 1997, IEEE, 0-7 803-4 122-8

[9] Buneman P., "Mathematics in the Archaelogical and Historical Sciences", 1971, F Hodson Edinburgh Univ Press, Edinburgh, UK, pp 387–395.

[10] Gascuel O, Steel M, "Neighbor-joining revealed", 2006, Mol Biol Evol 23:1997–2000.

[11] Aitken AC, "On least squares and linear combinations of observations", 1935, Proc R Soc Edinburgh A 55:42–48

[12] Vinh S, von Haeseler, "A Shortest triplet clustering: Reconstructing large phylogenies using representative sets", 2005, BMC Bioinf 6:92

[13] Jukes T, Cantor C, "Mammalian Protein Metabolism", 1969, H Munro (Academic, Waltham, MA), pp 21–132.

[14] Beyer W, Stein M, Smith T, Ulam S, "A molecular sequence metric and evolutionary trees", 1974, Math Biosci 19:9–25

[15] Atteson K, "The performance of neighbor-joining methods of phylogenetic reconstruction", 1999, Algorithmica 25:251–278

[16] Susko E, Inagaki Y, Roger A, "On inconsistency of the neighbor-joining, least squares, and minimum evolution estimation when substitution processes are incorrectly modeled", 2004, Mol Biol Evol 21:1629–1642

[17] Pardi F, Guillemot S, Gascuel O, "Robustness of phylogenetic inference based on minimum evolution", 2010, Bull Math Biol 72:1820–1839

[18] Rzhetsky A, Nei M, "A simple method for estimating and testing minimum evolution trees", 1992, Mol Biol Evol 9:945–967

[19] De Soete G, "A least squares algorithm for fitting additive trees to proximity data", 1983, Psychometrika 48:621–626

[20] Mihaescu R, Pachter L, "Combinatorics of least squares trees", 2008, Proc Natl Acad Sci USA 105:13206–13211

[21] Vatanjeet Singh, Aman Nag, Ekambir Sidhu," High Gain Ultra Wide Band (UWB) Multi Resonant Antenna for Biomedical Applications, Security Purposes and Drug Detection", 2016, IEEE, 978-1-4673-9338-6

[22] Nima Aliakbarinodehi, Giovanni De Micheli, Sandro Carrara," Optimized Electrochemical Detection of Anti-Cancer Drug by Carbon Nanotubes or Gold Nanoparticles", 2015, IEEE, 978-1-4799-8229-5

[23] Patricia Vazquez, Conor O'Mahony, Joseph O'Brien, Grégoire Herzog," Microneedle sensor for voltammetric drug detection in physiological fluids", 2014, IEEE, 978-1-4799-0162-3

[24] Pedro R. Gomes, C. S. Lima, Filomena O. Soares, J. H. Correia," Automatic Continuous ECG Monitoring System for Over-drug Detection in Brugada Syndrome", 2011, IEEE, 978-1-4244-4122-8

[25] Daniela De Venuto, Sandro Carrara, Andrea Cavallini, Giovanni De Micheli," pH Sensing with Temperature Compensation in a Molecular Biosensor for Drugs Detection", 2011, IEEE, 978-1-61284-914-0

[26] S. Sara Ghoreishizadeh, Camilla Baj-Rossi, Sandro Carrara, Giovanni De Micheli", Nano-Sensor and Circuit Design for Anti-Cancer Drug Detection", 2011, IEEE, 978-1-4577-0422-2

[27] M. Koutalonis, E.J. Cook, J.A. Griffiths, J.A. Horrocks, C. Gent, S. Pani, L. George, S. Hardwick, R. Speller", Designing an In-Field System for Illicit Drug Detection Using X-Ray Diffraction", 2009, IEEE, 9781-4244-3962-1

[28] R.Sindhu and V.Bhuvaneswari "Constructing Evolutionary Tree [Phylogeny] using BRICH Algorithm", Published in Journal of Karpagam JCS, 2009, Vol 3, Issue 4

[29] Go-Ebi, Embl-Ebi, et.al., "The Gene Ontology (GO) Database And Informatics Resource", Published in Journal of Nucleic Acid Research, 2003,Vol 32, pp 258-261

[30] Naruya Saitou And Masatoshi Nei "The Neighbor-Joining Method: A New Method For Reconstructing Phylogenetic Trees", Published in Journal of Molecular Biology Evolution 1981, Vol 4, Issue 4, pp 406 -425

[31] David Bryant and Vincent Moulton et.al., "Neighbor-Net: An Agglomerative Method For The Construction Of Phylogenetic Networks", Published in Journal of Molecular Biology Evolution,2003, Vol 21, Issue 2, pp 255-265

[32] A.Dereeper, V. Guignon, G. Blanc, S. Audic, S. Buffet, F. Chevenet, J.-F. Dufayard, S. Guindon, V. Lefort, M. Lescot, J.-M. Claveriel and O. Gascuel, "Phylogeny.Fr: Robust Phylogenetic Analysis for the Non-Specialist", Published in Journal of Nucleic Acids Research, 2008, Vol 36

[33] Scott V. Edwards and Liang Liu et.al "High-resolution species trees without concatenation", Published in Journal of Proceeding National Academy of Science, 2007 Vol 104, Issue 14 pp: 5936-5941

[34] Gregory E. Jordan and William.H, "Phylowidget: Web-Based Visualizations For The Tree Of Life", Published in Journal of Bioinformatics Ontology 2008, Vol 24, Issue 14, pp 1641-1642

[35] Fabio Pardi1 and Olivier Gascuel, "Combinatorics of Distance-Based Tree Inference", Published in Journal of Proceeding National Academy of Science, 2012, Vol 109, Issue 41, pp 16443-16448

[36] Georgios A. Pavlopoulos, Theodoros G Soldatos et.al. "A reference guide for tree analysis and visualization" 2010 Research journal of BioData Mining

[37] John P. Huelsenbeck and Fredrik Ronquist "Mr Bayes 3: Bayesian Phylogenetic inference under mixed models", Published in bioinformatics oxford journals 2003 Vol 19, Issue 12, pp-1572-1574

[38] Satya S. Sahoo, Olivier Bodenreider , Joni L. Rutter , Karen J. Skinner, Amit P. Sheth, "An ontology-driven semantic mashup of gene and biological pathway information: Application to the domain of nicotine dependence", 2008, Journal of Biomedical Informatics, 41 pp. 752–765

[39] Ziheng Yang "Phylogenetic Analysis Using Parsimony And Likelihood Methods", Published in Journal of Molecular Evolution, 1996, Vol 42, pp 294–307

[40] M. Sharmila, Dr.V.Bhuvaneswari, "Phylogeny Visualization Using Ontology Approach", 2014, IEEE